Poetic Reflections
by Mr. Nobody

Poetic Reflections by Mr. Nobody

For better or verse

James H. Tait

AuthorHouse™
1663 Liberty Drive
Bloomington, IN 47403
www.authorhouse.com
Phone: 1-800-839-8640

© 2011 by James H. Tait. All rights reserved.

No part of this book may be reproduced, stored in a retrieval system, or transmitted by any means without the written permission of the author.

First published by AuthorHouse   08/31/2011

ISBN: 978-1-4567-9686-0 (sc)
ISBN: 978-1-4567-9688-4 (ebk)

Printed in the United States of America

Any people depicted in stock imagery provided by Thinkstock are models, and such images are being used for illustrative purposes only.
Certain stock imagery © Thinkstock.

This book is printed on acid-free paper.

Because of the dynamic nature of the Internet, any web addresses or links contained in this book may have changed since publication and may no longer be valid. The views expressed in this work are solely those of the author and do not necessarily reflect the views of the publisher, and the publisher hereby disclaims any responsibility for them.

CONTENTS

Ode To The Bard	1
Wishes For A Beautiful Year	2
A Second Chance	4
Live For Today	5
Do It Now	6
Good Companions	7
People	9
Life's Journey	10
Hope	11
To My Love At Christmas	12
New Year Resolution	13
Who Am I?	14
Marriage	15
I Hate Funerals	17
Happy Birthday, Brown-Eyes	18
Janet And John	20
Sport For Old Folk	22
Diana, Queen Of Hearts	24
A Housewife's Warning	26
Tomorrow Is Another Day	29
My Garden	30
Revised Nursery Rhymes	32
Winter	35
Pollution Pollution	36
A Telephone Call To A Friend	37

ODE TO THE BARD

To write, or not to write?

That is the question.

Whether it is best to unleash the mind and let the reader suffer
the slings and arrows of inflated egos or open up a can of worms
and let them die so as to avoid the heartaches; or suffer more
calamities and make us bear those ills we have
against others we do not know.
Thus conscience does make cowards of us all.

Discard all doubt, dear friends, let not your resolution
be sicklied o'er with the pale cast of thought.

Take quill in hand and with staunch heart
let words and thoughts spill out

so that we may share your history
and heap praise upon your memory!

WISHES FOR A BEAUTIFUL YEAR

Happiness, a year without care
The sun on your face, a soft breeze in your hair
A perfumed garden full of bright flowers
Camellias and pinks, and rose covered bowers.

A leafy glade with gold glinting through
Soft grass underfoot, a sky coloured blue.
Meadows of buttercups and sweet smelling clover
Visions of England, and the white cliffs of Dover.

Barefoot strolls on a soft sandy beach
A sail on the bay, a iced drink within reach
A glass of champagne, Chablis or brandy
A Pimms No.1 or a lemonade shandy!

A creamy ice cone ready for licking
Plump juicy berries just right for the picking
Ham off the bone, a rich chocolate gateau
Smoked salmon and oysters, eaten al fresco.

Trees like umbrellas, rain like warm dew.
Lingering sunsets of red orange hue
Bright starlight nights, with the moon climbing higher
A cosy armchair, a crackling log fire

A symphony orchestra playing Gershwin or Greig
A best selling novel you just cannot leave
Hobbies and interests to pass time of day
Satisfaction at work, and pleasure in play.

WISHES FOR A BEAUTIFUL YEAR (cont.)

Friends and companions to confide in and trust
Knowing their words will be unbiased and just
The joy of a baby, lying soft skinned on a rug
Or asleep in your arms, all warm and snug.

A sweet face to kiss, a small body to touch
Dimples to smile at, tiny fingers to clutch.
A grandchild or more, to watch grow with pride,
Family bonded, love never denied!

Joy and contentment, all things that please
Laughter and smiles, a mind quite at ease.
A home filled with happiness and all of life's best
Sometimes quite noisy sometimes at rest,
Days of good health, good fortune and love
A year and a lifetime of all the above!

A SECOND CHANCE

With every passing moment we've the chance to start again
A chance to pledge ourselves anew, like sunshine after rain.
A chance to go on hoping when everything goes wrong,
So start again with trust and joy, and in your heart a song.

With each new hour beginning there's a chance to put things right.
To cast out every selfish thought and put it out of sight,
To put aside a grievance and help those who are sad,
And by the time the hour has gone you will feel so glad.

With every new day dawning, think of other people's plight
So try to solve their problems, turn darkness into light.
Consider other people, help them along the way,
You will find that life's worth living as you journey through each day.

With every month that comes along, give every man a smile
Let tears turn into laughter and things will be worthwhile.
Turn hatred into loving, give peace to all the old
And you will find true friends around more precious than pure gold

Poetic Reflections by Mr. Nobody

LIVE FOR TODAY

So much of life is wasted: we think it's there to stay,
We take it all for granted, it's just another day.
So often have we heard it said, "We'll do that tomorrow."
But only now is what we have, tomorrow's not to borrow.
It's only when today has gone, we find it much too late
To do the things we should have done instead of let them wait.

Our eyes will close at bedtime, with no guarantee or warning
That they will open up again, and see another morning.
Those hasty words you uttered and wish you left unsaid,
make sure that you retract them before you go to bed.
Think of all the misery if things are left undone
If never on the morrow you wake to see the sun.

The one you loved and left behind will forever and a day
Not forget the words you've spoken, the last they heard you say.
And so in times of anger, as we often sometimes do
We say the things that later we have the cause to rue.
Waste not a single moment, don't cock a snook at fate,
Now's the time to take it back, for tomorrow's much too late.

James H. Tait

DO IT NOW

If with pleasure you are viewing
Any work a man is doing,
If you like him,
or you love him, tell him now.

Don't withhold your approbation
Till the parson makes oration
And he lies with snowy lilies on his brow,
For no matter how you shout it, he won't really care about it,
he won't know how many teardrops you have shed.

If you think some praise is due him, now is the time to tell him
For he cannot read the tombstone when he's dead.
More than fame and more than money
Is the comment kind and sunny
And the hearty, warm approval of a friend.
For it gives to life a savour, and makes you stronger, braver
And it gives you heart and spirit to the end.

If he earns your praise, bestow it.
If you like him, let him know it.
Let the words of true encouragement be said.
Do not wait till life is over
And he is underneath the clover
For he cannot read his tombstone when he's dead.

GOOD COMPANIONS

I am aged.
I am weary.
I am alone.
I stop. I look ahead.
An empty desert
Stretching to the horizon,
Motionless, treeless, waterless.

I look up.
Grey sky. Birdless.
Still. Unsympathetic.
Dull as my life.

I look back.
I see a fresh grave
A headstone, marble white.
My husband's name upon it.

I look ahead.
Nothing.
Should I end my journey here?
Rest my tired bones,
Lie down and sleep?
Let the desert claim me?

Behind me
Two figures rise from the dust
And approach.
Strong hands lift me up.
I ask their names.
"Hope," said one
"Faith" said the other.

GOOD COMPANIONS (cont.)

We will be your companions.
Let us travel with you
And lighten your steps.
Beyond the desert
Is a green oasis
Where you will feel refreshed.

So I journeyed on
With my two protectors.
The desert blossomed
The sky turned blue
Filled with birdsong
And I found love again.

PEOPLE

Some people expect very little
Some people hope for much
Some people are self-reliant
And others need a crutch.
People are so different
With varied hopes and dreams
Ambitions that they cherish
While striving for the means!
Now life is full of pitfalls
For the unwary and the meek
Weathering those stormy squalls
Needs a determined streak.
But some folk lack the confidence
And the strength to battle through
They often need encouragement
And a smile from me and you
To show that they can achieve success
And all that they desire
If they do not let despondency
Quench their ambition's fire.
So surely it's important
And a kindly thing to do
To extend a hand of friendship
And give a nod or two
In support of those around us
Who are fearful of the fray
For they are also on the journey
That will end for us one day.

LIFE'S JOURNEY

Travelling through life is like touring the Earth
It needs good navigation from the moment of birth
So it is not too surprising if we oft lose our way
But help is at hand if we kneel down and pray.

Dark tangled paths crisscross the land
To tread safely through you need God's guiding hand
Mountains and rivers need to be crossed
And deserts and jungles, where one can get lost

The road to salvation is not easy to find
Dangers abound which can disturb every mind
But you can step confidently right to the end
If you allow God to be your escort and friend.

HOPE

The history of Man is full of contradiction
Each chapter tells of war and friction.
Yet prayers of peace and love abound
And the word of God is all around.

TO MY LOVE AT CHRISTMAS

Once again it's Christmas
And another verse is due
To express my thoughts for all that passed
And declare my love anew.
But what more can I say to you
I have never said before?
Different expressions that ring true
Without sounding like a bore.
Is there another word for love
To describe the way I feel?
A word that fits like hand in glove
Or a spoke within a wheel.

Consult a dictionary if you will
And try with all your might
But love is the emotion that I feel
And the only word that's right.
So forgive me if I repeat myself
But love is the only word to say
Pledged in sickness and in health
As on our wedding day.

I could not have had a better wife
To share my life all through.
With every passing year that flies
You prove that fact is true.
A true companion and good friend
You have been more than I could ask
So I will be grateful to the end
If you'd complete the task!

Poetic Reflections by Mr. Nobody

NEW YEAR RESOLUTION

Life is so busy, and time seems to fly
And it is hard to keep up with the year going by
There is so much to do, so much to remember
From January right through to December
But each fresh New Year we must give a thought
To all the past years and what they have brought.

Life brings its problems, as each one will know,
And we need courage, the older we grow.
But when we look back we cannot deny
The black clouds above us have always passed by
Brightening us with the warmth of the sun
And letting us know another battle's been won.

We have had our good times, with good fortune too
And so we must look forward to the year that is new.
We must tackle each day while learning to cope
With every new problem with prayer and hope,
Taking strength from each other, and giving our love.
We will survive with help from above.

To all my dear friends, this thought goes to you
On this New Year's Day, now almost due,
We reap what we sow, and so it should be,
For caring for others knits each family.
Love and true friendship should shine from each door
With comfort and goodness always in store.
And always about you, please bear in mind
Are strong moral values that will never unbind.

WHO AM I?

I am a Man, born of Woman
From the seed of Man.
Am I thus a child of God?
I do not know,
Though the Scriptures tell me so
But they were written long ago.

Please help, I want to understand
Who I am, and what I am.
I am confused. What is the truth?
Do I have a soul within
Implanted by some immortal hand?
Or am I only flesh, with feet of clay
That when I die will just decay.

It grieves my mind to suppose
That eventually I will decompose,
With nothing left to journey on
Into further time, however long,
Not leaving any part of me intact
And without the knowledge of the fact
That there is more to life than death

It seems the mystery will remain
Until my mortal race is run.
When darkness falls upon my brain
Will my spirit find the sun?

MARRIAGE

If you took the time to think about your married life
When you are faced with a problem, or dealing with strife
When the air is so tense it can be cut with a knife
You may suddenly wonder why you became man and wife

The answer is not easy when you are having a fight
Or the baby is screaming night after night
And whatever you do never seems to be right.
The temptation exists to go out and get tight.
So what is the secret? How do you cope?

The Archbishop cannot help you, nor will the Pope
If you don't work together you have not a hope
And your marriage will be on a slippery slope.

The truth is so simple-it is all about sharing
Of giving and loving, of helping and caring
Supporting each other when life become wearing
And mending the hurt when hearts feel like tearing.

When all's said and done, true love is the way
To bring forth blue skies and banish the gray
Caring for each other day after day
Helping your partner keep troubles at bay

To sum it all up, the message is clear
People in love have nothing to fear
Just comfort each other when the odd tear is near
And your marriage should last for year after year.

James H. Tait

MARRIAGE (cont.)

Of course I must say it helps if you choose
The right sort of partner who holds the same views
Who doesn't sniff glue or goes on the booze
Or provides Sunday newspapers with scandalous news!

A couple must know before they get wed
There is more to marriage than sharing a bed
If that's all that matters there is trouble ahead
And before very long the marriage is dead.

My advice to young lovers is don't be afraid
Your marriage will last if strong foundations are laid
Be kind to each other and love will not fade
And if you keep to the vows that both of you made.

Poetic Reflections by Mr. Nobody

I HATE FUNERALS

I hate funerals.
Crematoria are such cold and sombre places
When filled with sad and tearful faces.
Each mournful figure blackly dressed
Shoulders slumped and head depressed
Bowed with heavy weight of grief
So shocked by death, which like a thief
Snatched a loved one from their side
And left them pained and empty eyed.

Dulled senses deaf to pious word
The vicar's droning voice unheard,
Tired minds blank, unheeding
No comfort gained from Bible reading.

Along the pews the downcast eyes
Shed slow, hot tears, while painful sighs
Echo loud above the whispered prose
Until mourners rise in hunched phose   (prose)
To sing in wavering uncertain tones
Hymns designed to soothe the groans
But merely heighten the despair
Which leaden fill the cheerless air.

And finally, so dreadful as it goes,
As brains are numbed and hearts are froze
The coffin slowly sinks and slides away
Silent except for moans for it to stay.
With that spent life burn all the dreams
And nothing left but stifled screams.

∽ James H. Tait ∽

HAPPY BIRTHDAY, BROWN~EYES

I know the house is full of books
With paper piled on high
And clothes not always put on hooks,
Which give you cause to sigh.

Faults I have, I'll not deny
You have every right to curse
But I hope you will find a kiss for me
When you have read this verse.

I know I am often boring
With moods that hardly charm
But my heart is always dancing
When you are on my arm.

I am hardly built like Tarzan
With muscles to be proud
But in our urban jungle
I will roar my love out loud

You were always my sweetheart
From our teenage years
I loved you from the very start
And I do not care who hears!

I am not a handsome film star
Nor yet a millionaire
I am just an ordinary person
With little brain to spare

Poetic Reflections by Mr. Nobody

HAPPY BIRTHDAY, BROWN-EYES (cont.)

But of one thing I am certain
If you need someone to care
I am just the very man for you
Your joys and tears to share

So when I am in the garden
Or growling like a bear
Let not your heart be hardened
But remember how I care!

JANET AND JOHN

I first heard the story of Janet and John
When on Grandma's lap I sat upon.
They were middle class children with middle class names
Going to school and playing their games
Doing the things a child likes to do
And having adventures that really seemed true.

I suppose I grew up with Janet and John
Reading their stories until my schooldays had gone.
In the end, they became real, I knew them so well
And I was jealous of John, if the truth I should tell.
I had fallen for Janet, so pretty and good
I'd have changed places with John, if only I could!

I hated to read how they played together
For I knew I'd love Janet forever and ever!
There were pictures of them on page after page
Each one I turned over I became full of rage!
John was a wimp, a dolt and a bore
Why did not Janet show him the door?

As I tossed in my bed night after night
I cursed the author, and hoped he would write
That John had come to a sticky end
And Janet was looking for another good friend.
But how could the writer know of my need?
He only wrote stories for children to read.

Janet and John were only fiction
He wasn't to know that I had been smitten.
So I kept my emotions all to myself
And placed all the books on a very high shelf.

Poetic Reflections by Mr. Nobody

JANET AND JOHN (cont.)

That's where they stayed for a very long while
Though everyone wondered why I never smiled.

The years passed by until I grew old,
And then one fine day, lo and behold,
As I walked down the road, suddenly she,
Real flesh and blood, was looking at me!
I could not believe it, I must have gone mad!
The years disappeared, and I was back as a lad.

Now here she was, Janet without John,
And wondering why I was staring so long.
While wild thoughts were going round in my head
She stepped even closer, and boldly said
"Do you know from somewhere? You are looking quite red!"
Now how could I tell her I had loved her for years
And seeing her now almost reduced me to tears?
So I just shook my head with a smile so polite
With my fists clenched so very tight.
I looked deep into her eyes and then walked slowly away
But now I keep wondering day after day.
If Janet had escaped from her fairy book life
Had John escaped too, and was she his wife?
I wished I had been braver, with the question to ask
Though I was afraid of the answer, and be taken to task.

The moral of this tale is sadly true
Growing up in the real world is what people must do
Fairy stories are fine as long as we know
The characters are imagined, and not really so.

SPORT FOR OLD FOLK

Another birthday? Congratulations! But at seventy-six
I wonder now how you will get your kicks?
I have tried to think what you can play
To keep you young and fit and gay.

Did I say gay? I am very sorry
I don't wish to offend. I really mean 'jolly'
Now, let's think. Football's out. You'd get a stitch
Running up and down the soccer pitch.

Cricket's no good if your eyes have gone
You would not see the wicket from silly mid on.
Rugby, I am afraid, is too physical a game
After a scrum you would finish up lame

Tennis? If you ever tried playing on court
You would surely lose each set to naught.
What about golf? No good at all!
You would find every bunker and lose every ball.

Bowls may be better, but in bowling the wood
You must bend the knees, if only you could!
And your problem would be in hitting the jack
You would spend all the game clutching your back.

Angling? I know you loved fishing
But you would only catch cold, so no point in wishing
So that's put an end to all outdoor sports
And posing for pictures in tee shirt and shorts.

Poetic Reflections by Mr. Nobody

SPORT FOR OLD FOLK (cont.)

That leaves indoors. So, what can you do?
A sport or a game you think may suit you.
Sorry. Not that. That is far too exciting.
Not even if you turned down the lighting.

Your darling wife in negligee and lace
Would only make your heartbeat race.
Far too risky to have a floor show
Or glimpse a part uncovered torso.

Those days have gone. I am afraid you will find
The only sex now must stay in your mind.
Here is an idea, though it is not quite the same,
You could sit close together and play a nice game.

Make a weak cup of cocoa to settle yourself
And find something quiet that won't tax your health.
How about cards? Now, that is not hard labour.
A game like 'Snap' or "Beat Your Neighbour".

No. Not strip poker. In Y—fronts and vest
You really would not be looking your best!
What about draughts? That can be thrilling.
Tiddleywinks too, you could try if you're willing

Of course there's the telly. Cartoons can be fun
Jackanory and Woodentops start about one.
The choice is yours, there is so much to view
But whatever you do, a Happy Birthday to you!

DIANA, QUEEN OF HEARTS

The blow hit hard. A dagger thrust.
The tragic journey. The end unjust
We heard the news with disbelief
Numbness first, before the grief
Inflicted burning, searing pain
Through every sinew, every vein,
Which tore our hearts, and left us weak
Gasping air, unfit to speak.

How could we lose Diana
In such a stupid violent manner?
She paid the price for senseless greed
No value placed upon her need
For privacy or peace of mind.
Even as she sat and dined
The vultures waited, eager still
To close in quickly for the kill.

And so it proved. Their deadly game
A blood-sport, truly, to their shame.
A princess hunted to her end
Along with dear devoted friend.
We mourn their deaths, so undeserved
We shed our tears, quite unreserved.
But anger, too, is mixed with pain
That they will never laugh again.

Scorn and envy played their part
To cause the damage to each heart.
No doubt Diana was ill-used
In many way. Hurt and abused
By those in whom she placed her trust.
Her confidence ground down to dust

DIANA, QUEEN OF HEARTS (cont.)

By arrogance and snobbishness
From the Establishment. who even less
Failed to appreciate her real worth

The common people of the earth
Recognised it and how she cared
About them all. She even dared
To touch those with Aids and leprosy,
Showed compassion, love and charity
Not displayed by those who sneered.
Those lesser mortals who always feared
That they would catch a dread disease
While Diana comforted and laughed with ease.
Disregarding each affliction,
Dispensing care and true affection.

No wonder children loved her so
She made each tiny spirit glow.
A true princess, but with the common touch
She is missed, so much, so much.
To be Queen of Hearts she deeply yearned
It was a title she so surely earned

James H. Tait

A HOUSEWIFE'S WARNING

Married life is busy
With little time to rest
So it isn't very easy
To be always full of zest.
Each day those household chores
Have made me feel like screaming.
Making beds and cleaning floors
Was not what I was dreaming
When snuggled to a manly chest
I surrendered to his words of fire
Those promises he would do his best
To fulfil my heart's desire.

I sealed my future with a kiss.
I imagined life so rosy.
Sunny days and nights of bliss
In a cottage warm and cosy
But fairy tales do not come true
Or not often, as you know
And dreams disperse like morning dew
Or melting springtime snow.
I am afraid I soon discovered
My man around the house
Changed from ardent lover
When I became his spouse.

No longer flowers strong with scent
Are pressed into my arms
Nor romantic notes with sweet intent
Beguiling with his charms.
His gifts are now his underwear
Left strewn upon the floor

⁀ Poetic Reflections by Mr. Nobody ⁀

A HOUSEWIFE'S WARNING (cont.)

Dirty laundry everywhere
As he dashes out the door
He has left the bathroom like a wreck
But he has not time right now
Except to plant a hasty kiss
Upon my perspiring brow!

No time to screw the lid back on the paste
Or wipe up where he's slopped
He's late for work and must make haste
Or he would have stayed and mopped!
So to all you ladies who would be wives
I will leave you with this thought.
Do not expect romantic lives
For you'll be surely caught.
Whatever you may dream or hope
That your marriage will be bliss
It may be like an East End Soap
That you would rather miss.

Nor is it easy once you've wed
To admit your passion's died
And many tears may be shed
Before the knot's untied.
So be sure you know the man you've wed
Don't be dazzled by his smile
Just make sure you're not misled
By his flattery or his style.
Sweet tender words you'll no doubt hear
But here is good reason for the charm
Let me state it very clear
Though the thought may cause alarm.

James H. Tait

A HOUSEWIFE'S WARNING (cont.)

A man will need a cook and nurse
As well as eager lover.
A housemaid, gardener, and maybe worse,
A companion for his mother!
So I urge you now to sit and think
Before you take your vows
You may not get the pearls and mink
That you are dreaming of right now.
Instead a Hoover and a stove
May be bestowed on you to treasure
While hubby slips away to rove
And enjoy himself at leisure!

TOMORROW IS ANOTHER DAY

We must not dwell upon our past
Now that most of life has spun
We cannot bring back what has gone
Nor regret what we've not done.

Nor should we look too far ahead
With hopes beyond our reach
For often they will be scattered
Like pebbles on the beach.

The present is what matters
We have it in our hands.
Let it not slip through our fingers
Like wasted grains of sand.

The future is uncertain
And not for us to know
But before the final curtain
Let love and friendship grow.

Enjoy today, each moment of the hours
Use wisely and purposefully
Take pleasure in your garden flowers
And forget mortality.

MY GARDEN

I am a simple soul, I like to garden
I always will, till arteries harden.
I spend most days among my blooms
Rather than walk through empty rooms.

Filled with laughter, once they were
My heart filled with love for her.
My darling wife for almost sixty years
Always there through my careers.

Through Navy days and RAF,
Pledged to me until my death.
I thought I ever would be blessed.
Until fate tricked me with cruel jest.

It took her first, without warning,
One summer's day, in early morning.
So now I garden, planting flowers
In her memory, and to pass the hours.

Myosotis, or Forget-Me-Nots (as if I could),
Bluebells, remembering long walks in the woods
Her favourite roses, pansies and begonia
Though they make me feel still lonelier.

MY GARDEN (cont.)

Hydrangeas, clematis and pink camellia
Praying Thyme would be a healer.
Like all the flowers, her perfume lingers
While the days slip sadly through my fingers.

One day there will be another garden
If my sins the Lord will pardon,
And my love and I will be together
Hand in hand in golden heather.

James H. Tait

REVISED NURSERY RHYMES

Humpty Dumpty sat on a wall
Humpty Dumpty had a great fall
All the King's soldiers and all the King's men
Had scrambled egg for breakfast.

Curly locks, curly locks
Wilt thou be mine?
Thou shall not wash the dishes
Nor feed the swine
Not till after the wedding, anyway!

Pease pudding hot
Pease pudding cold
Pease pudding in a pot
Nine days old.
Can you really fancy it
When it's turned to mould?

Higgledy Piggledy, my black hen
She lays eggs for gentlemen
Sometimes nine and sometimes ten
Full of salmonella, my fat hen.

Hickory Dickory Dock
The mouse ran up the clock
The clock struck one
The mouse has gone
Turned into a pumpkin.

⚘ Poetic Reflections by Mr. Nobody ⚘

REVISED NURSERY RHYMES (cont.)

There was a little girl
Who had a little curl
Right in the middle of her forehead
When she was good she was very, very good
And when she was bad, oh boy!

Sing a song of sixpence,
A pocket full of rye
It does not make a lot of sense
But who can judge? Not I! Not I!

Jack and Jill went up the hill
To fetch a pail of water
Jill came down with half a crown
For doing what she didn't oughter.

Diddle, diddle dumpling
My son John
Went to bed with his trousers on
One shoe off and one shoe on
Drunk as a lord, my son John!

Dr Foster went to Gloucester
In a shower of rain
He stepped in a puddle right up to his middle
Part of the NHS down the drain!

Rub a dub dub
Three men in a tub.
How do you think they got there?
The butcher, the baker, the candlestick maker
Fancied a bath all together!

⚘ 33 ⚘

⁓ James H. Tait ⁓

REVISED NURSERY RHYMES (cont.)

Mary, Mary, quite contrary
How does your garden grow?
With acid rain, pollution too,
Not enough veg to make good stew.

Pat a cake, pat a cake, baker's man
Make love to me now as quick as you can
Pat me and stroke me and fill me with glee
And put a bun in the oven
For you and me!

Yankee Doodle came to town
Riding on a pony
She stuck a feather in her cap
To try to win an election.
Poor Hillary Clinton!

Little Miss Muffet
Had ordered a buffet
To eat on her wedding day
Along came a soldier
And sat down beside her
And took her hunger away!

There was an old woman who lived in a shoe
She had so many children she did not know what to do
She gave then some broth without any bread
And laced it with arsenic that killed them all dead.

Poetic Reflections by Mr. Nobody

WINTER

Mother is crying, a desolate sound,
Father is dying, hospital gowned,
A Sister attending all through the night
Teardrops descending on to cheeks wetly bright.

Mother is weeping, a desperate sound
Father is sleeping, cold underground.
Snowflakes are blending in a cover of white
Teardrops descending on to earth shiny bright

James H. Tait

POLLUTION POLLUTION

Pollution. Pollution
What is the solution?
Pollution. pollution
Is poisoning the nation.
Fouling the towns, tainting the villages.
Nuclear waste, chemical spillages,
Factory stench, industrial smoke.
Is it not time for ordinary folk
To damn the contamination and the degeneration
That is damaging the lungs of the whole population.

Pollution, Pollution
It makes me despair
That so many Governments don't seem to care
That rivers and lakes, the air and the sea
Are filled with poisons that harm you and me.
Pollution, Pollution, it is lying out there
Where ever you look it is everywhere,
Dirty and smelly, fumes deadly to breathe,
Bring fatalities and the reason to grieve.

Poetic Reflections by Mr. Nobody

A TELEPHONE CALL TO A FRIEND

Since I have not called for a while
I thought your number I would dial
To see if you were still OK
Before I sent a small bouquet
In memory of those golden days
When we romped care free in summer haze
In our youth before the war.
We danced barefoot along the shore
With eyes for only one another
Attention focussed on each other.

I was smitten from the day we met
When you spied me soaking wet
Splashing madly in a gutter pool
While on the way to primary school.
You laughed so much at my damp state
That for assembly we were late,
But afterwards as bold as brass
I walked you all the way from class
And even then I somehow knew
There would be no other one than you.

I was ten and you were nine
I really thought you were divine!
And though my chums thought me a fool
I always waited after school.
And so begun our love affair
No time for others could we spare.
We laughed and played until our teens
When we learned what heartache means.

A TELEPHONE CALL TO A FRIEND (cont.)

Wrapped in each other we failed to sense
That a deadly war would soon commence
Or the threat to our future the Nazis posed
With the conquest of Europe that Hitler proposed.
Your parents decided to take you away
Though for how long no one could say.
With the threat overhead it was the best thing to do
To escape all the bombing, and start life anew.
We were so young how could we guess
That the parting would leave our lives in a mess?
Soon you sailed on a liner, Canada bound
Leaving me desolate, in misery drowned.

I missed you so badly it was hard to think straight
But I knew in my heart I would have a long wait.
I had to do something to help end the war
The fulfilment of dreams was worth fighting for.
I joined the Air Force as soon as I could
But just a year later I crashed in a wood.
You had written so often, so desperately,
Each tearful letter praying for my safety
That I could not inform you of what had occurred
I told all my friends not to utter a word.

I was a mess; my recovery was slow
And for a time it was touch and go.
My limbs finally healed but my burnt skin did not
The scars on my face could not be forgot.
Nor would my fingers ever work properly again
It was a hard effort just grasping a cane.
One look in the mirror left my dreams truly shattered
I wanted no pity: it was your future that mattered.

≈ Poetic Reflections by Mr. Nobody ≈

A TELEPHONE CALL TO A FRIEND (cont.)

How could I ask you to share my wrecked life
I could not expect you to become my dear wife.
I wrote to you harshly, not telling the truth
Pouring cold water, sounding aloof.
The war had changed me. I had met someone new
And I regretted to say I no longer loved you.
I imagined your face with each lie that I wrote
And it pained me so much to post off the note.
It seemed an eternity before I received your reply
Your sad puzzled words left me wanting to die.
Yet your message was brave, so dignified too
Not unexpected from the girl that I knew.
You wished me good luck and said you would stay
Forever in Canada and forget yesterday.

The next several years are worth hardly a mention
I was discharged with a disablement pension.
When the war ended I bought a small flat
Alone with my memories and a little black cat!
I dreamt of you often, my mind going round
Praying that happiness you would have found.
Then, by chance I met an old friend
Who was going to Ottawa and said he would send
Any news he could find of your family and self
If you were happy, and in a state of good health.

I waited impatiently for his mail to return
Wondering if there was any good news to learn.
The letter that came filled me with gladness
Though I cannot deny also some sadness.
You had married a doctor and given birth to a son
It consoled me a little for the lies I had spun.

≈ 39 ≈

James H. Tait

A TELEPHONE CALL TO A FRIEND (cont.)

I was happy for you, though the news also pained
For what I had lost the doctor had gained.
At least you had found some contentment at last
And most of your heartbreak was a thing of the past.
My friend settled near you and was able to write
To keep me assured you were doing all right.
What I did not expect was his confession to you
That back in the war he was part of my crew.
Not only that but he was even more rash
Revealing the details of my near fatal crash.
When you heard the full story you knew I had lied
And without hesitation you flew to my side.
You knew your husband would understand
So we talked through the night, hand held in hand.
I was so thrilled to have you so near
Your touch was so soft, your face was so dear.

Of course all this happened long years ago
And time like the river has continued to flow.
I am still an old bachelor, living alone
But it's still always nice to pick up the 'phone
To speak to an old friend just for a chat
Talking of old times and this and that.
How is your weather? Have you had snow?
Did you manage last year your roses to grow?
I well remember those lovely blooms
You sent me to fill my dull old rooms
Though none compared in grace or form
With you, who took my heart by storm.
When I was young and full of glee
Every time you looked at me.

Poetic Reflections by Mr. Nobody

A TELEPHONE CALL TO A FRIEND (cont.)

Then I thought that on life's stage
We would dance until old age,
But that's all past. What pleases me
Is the love you have for your family.
I am content, for they look after you
Much more than ever I could do.

How am I now? I am not too bad
No reason now for feeling sad
Though I confess to feeling cold
It's part of growing old I'm told.
I also have a painful lumbar
So I'd find it hard to do the rhumba!
Mostly now I sit and read
Though stronger glasses now I need.
But it's a miracle they saved my sight
When I recall that tragic night
My plane caught fire above the town
And all my dreams came crashing down.

Did I hear you shed a tear?
Please don't cry. You must not fear
For me. So many men did not survive
Who would have wished to stay alive.
I am lucky to have been spared my life
And though I lost you as my wife
It is good to know you are still my friend
Who'll warm my heart until the end.

Goodnight, my dear. I will call again soon.
Now I shall sit quietly and gaze at the moon.

Lightning Source UK Ltd.
Milton Keynes UK
UKOW051355141011

180315UK00001B/53/P